BEYOND
STICKS AND STONES
Bullying, Cyberbullying, Abuse

By RJ Parker,
Criminologist, Author and Publisher

LARGE PRINT

BEYOND
STICKS AND STONES
Bullying, *Cyberbullying, Abuse*

By RJ Parker,
Criminologist, Author and Publisher

Copyrights © 2019
Second Edition

ISBN 978-1987902587

Published in Canada
LARGE PRINT

Copyrights

Table of Contents

DEDICATION

I dedicate this book to every child, teen, and adult who have been a victim of being bullied. Also, to my beautiful daughters, Amanda and Katie and Grandson, Parker.

To the bullies I only say, shame on you!!

"You have enemies? Good. That means you've stood up for something, sometime in your life."
- Winston Churchill

PINK SHIRT DAY

A day when people wear pink shirt to symbolize a stand against bullying, an idea that originated in Canada. It is celebrated on various dates around the world. The original event was organized by David Shepherd and Travis Price of Berwick, Nova Scotia, who in 2007 bought and distributed 50 pink shirts after male ninth grade student Chuck McNeill was bullied for wearing a pink shirt during the first day of school.

PROLOGUE

Are those who are bullied, victims? You bet!

Cyberbullying, harassment, embarrassing others, tormenting, threatening or humiliating, and spousal abuse are all considered 'bullying.' It happens to children, teens, and adults. It occurs in pre-school, elementary school, college, home, and in the workplace. It is apparent in all walks of life. Bullying occurs in every town, city, state, province and country, and it has many ugly faces.

But with today's technology, mobile phones, internet, Facebook, Twitter, Instagram, and a host of other platforms, I'm going to emphasize more on children, students, and teens, because that is where it commences and for most, carries over into their adult lives.

CHAPTER 1: THE PARADIGM OF BULLYING

Think back to the days when you were still young, going to school. Your mind was obviously not muddled with all of the daily problems that engulf an adult's mind, but it wasn't short of problems then. How many of us can claim to have been bullied in our younger lives? Or, how many of us can claim to have seen other children get bullied?

The term 'bullying' has a very comprehensive meaning, contrary to what most would believe. Some would argue that we are bullied even during our professional lives, when we are working our jobs and are forced to work harder, or perform different tasks by our bosses.

Bullying, like many other activities, has its varying degrees. Some bullies are content with pushing other students around; others are more exuberant and hit other students to force them to their will. However, there are those who get down to abusing others, forcing them to do shameful things, sometimes even before other students, or be beaten up. The problem is, that we learn the concept of bullying at such an early age that it never leaves our minds throughout our lives.

The general stereotype would have us believe that there are several kinds of students that you will meet. There is the 'nerd' crowd, which consists of studious, hard working students who keep their goals clear and are willing to get their heads down and study.

These children do not really involve themselves in sports or other sociable events, instead focusing on their studies exclusively and securing high marks. Then, there are the average students, who are involved in studies and sports. They might not be the top achievers in their classes, but they certainly aren't the lowest achievers either. They are, what you might call, mid-table students. Then, there are those who are generally not as good at studying but instead tend to focus their hearts and minds towards sports.

Such students are generally well built, with hulking bodies and strong personalities. Confidence flows through their veins, though their class performance isn't anywhere the satisfactory mark. Then, there is the lowest group; those who are not good in studies, nor any sports. So which group do we classify the bullies in?

Well, there is no set description of a bully, per se, except that you'd be hard pressed to find a bully who gets good grades in school. Again, common consensus is that those students who are not very good in sports and their studies are generally the ones that turn in to bullies. They might be physically healthy and stronger than the other students, hence their desire to pick on them. A bully is a person who makes use of physical force to manipulate other students. Funnily enough, the concept of bullying isn't a relatively new one. Instead, it's been around for ages.

If you were to believe history, it is said that Gaius Antonius and Mark Antony were also bullied by children who lived on their neighboring property. Hence, it is obvious that if bullying was around in the time of the Romans, it is generally an innate habit of humans.

Obviously, if you were stronger and physically more

powerful than another student, you would be willing to exercise your dominance on others. Because of their habits and spiteful nature, bullies don't even have a lot of friends, and the ones that they do, are usually friends with them because they are frightened of going against them. At least that's what the general consensus is.

However, our concept of bullying has been corrupted by popular media. Not all bullies are fat kids who love eating other students' lunches and beating them up. Their physical appearance doesn't really count as much as their activities.

Most of the time, children don't even bother telling their

parents that they are being bullied. This is because they do not want to be embarrassed before their parents. It is the innate nature of a child to make his parents proud, and when they find out that he is being bullied by another student, wouldn't the parents think that their child is not ready to stand up for himself? This is the first mistake that children make; not telling their parents. And this is what a bully thrives on. He knows that there's going to be no action against him. He knows that there isn't going to be anybody from a higher age group to stop him. And, even if there is somebody to stop him, bullies usually tell their victims not to share information or they will 'beat them up.' So, what about the kids who are bullied?

CHAPTER 2: KIDS WHO ARE BULLIED

In our minds, there is a common theory regarding the type of kids who are bullied. These are generally the physically weak kids, who are often picked upon by their stronger, healthier counterparts. However, that is not entirely true. Even though weak, 'nerdy' kids are picked upon quite often, there is no guarantee that bullies might not try their intimidating ways on other children, either male or female.

Previously, the primary reason for which kids were bullied was for their food or lunch money. Even though that kind of bullying still exists, it has evolved comparatively. Apart from wanting lunch money and food, bullies also make other demands. For instance, a lot of students report bullies have stolen their mobile phones, laptops, and other articles of clothing from them.

Despite their obvious frustration, these kids generally do not fight against their bullies. As a result of this, the bullies tend to prey on their fear, and their habit of staying quiet. This is one of the primary problems that most kids who are bullied suffer from. They do not want to tell their parents about the problems, nor do they wish to share these issues with somebody else. With the passage of time, these issues tend to creep in further and cause major problems in the long run throughout their lives, and the lives of those who are connected to such children.

Basically, kids are bullied in two different manners. They might be bullied publicly, in which case they are usually shamed and embarrassed before a crowd, causing them to become mentally distraught. However, if the bully is someone who also picks on others, the embarrassment might not be as big. The other kind of bullying is one in which the bully often picks on children when they are alone.

This is obviously the worst

kind of bullying, since children who are alone do not have anything to defend themselves with, and more importantly, tend to stay quiet about their ordeals. Some bullies also resort to molestation.

The problem amongst children is that they fail to realize the options available to them. Since they don't share, and also because most parents are usually unaware of the symptoms that might indicate whether their child is being bullied or not, these children are usually left to their own devices to suffer. Over the passage of time, this can turn out to be a very big problem for children, as constant bullying tends to eat away at their mental state, and ultimately, they have to resort to treatment, which often involves the use of anti-depressants.

CHAPTER 3: THE EFFECTS

The kids who are bullied are often left with some very bad memories that plague them for the rest of their lives. Very few children actually forget the moments of their childhood in which they were threatened, beaten up or intimidated.

It remains etched in to their memory for years to come, and usually doesn't go away until the time they see their bully pining away without a successful career while they build a successful life, at which point the shame, regret and anger is replaced by satisfaction and peace of mind.

However, kids who are bullied tend to develop certain characteristics that set them apart from other, healthy students. They often retreat in to themselves, becoming shy and withdrawn, and lose a good deal of their confidence.

Those kids who are bullied publicly are still able to deal with themselves, because they also see other kids being bullied by the same person. However, those who are bullied and threatened in hiding from bullies are often the worst sufferers. Compared to girls, boys are a lot more likely to be bullied in both physiological and psychological ways. As a result, most children who are bullied often tend to show obvious changes in their behaviors. Here are a few characteristics of kids who are bullied:

* Bullied children become very sensitive. Because they live in constant fear of the bully, these children are often quite sensitive to weird sounds in their surroundings, and might be taken aback at somebody shouting at them. A slight nudge to these children will seem as if somebody is trying to beat them.

* These children also become quite anxious. Again, because they are constantly living in fear of the bully, their mind and body adapts and often reaches a heightened

sense of awareness, hence making them anxious of their surroundings. These children are likely to fidget around quite a lot, and are unlikely to remain focused on one thing for a consistent period of time.

- The biggest characteristic of such students is that they become socially withdrawn. They are not interested in having conversations with others, primarily because they begin to think very little of themselves. More importantly, this also means that they do not show a lot of interest in any social events in schools or outdoors.

- Another obvious characteristic of bullied students is the amount of passiveness that they show. Such students aren't willing to stand up for themselves, nor do they like being in control. For instance, if the class has to select a group leader, these students won't even bother standing up because they don't mind who takes charge.

Often times, a child who has been bullied, if given the chance, will end up bullying others. This is primarily due psychological reasoning, because when they are bullied, they often respond with aggressiveness and anxiousness. And, because they are unable to truly process these feelings and combat them in a healthy way, they let these emotions out by channeling them on other children.

There have been many incidents in which students who have been bullied have resorted to committing suicide. In fact, in recent years, it's becoming an epidemic among our youth.

In some cases however, children who have been bullied lash out against their oppressors, turning on them violently.

For parents, it is important to look for signs of bullying in your child if he isn't telling you. They might make up pointless excuses to avoid going to school, might suffer from a very disturbed sleep and the most obvious of all: these students are likely to suffer from unexplained bruises. Upon query, you're likely to get answers such as, "I fell down," "I twisted my ankle," etc.

One prime example of bullying in the present day is Amanda Todd. Amanda Todd committed suicide on the October 10, 2012, after having been bullied, physically assaulted and blackmailed. She was also a victim of 'cyberbullying.' At the time of her death, Amanda was just 15 years old.

Some compromising pictures of hers were leaked on the internet, and she also made a video regarding her experiences, using flash cards to tell the audience about how she was suffering. Yet, nobody really paid attention to her story until she had committed suicide. Soon after, the video went viral, and international agencies launched investigations into her suicide.

Her death shows the power of bullying, and how it can be used in a variety of different ways to manipulate young children against their will. Kids who are bullied suffer from mental scars virtually throughout their lives. Some might even require therapy sessions in order to get their minds back in order. Amanda Todd's death serves as a major example in a lot of cases. Even though she was primarily bullied over the internet, it goes on to show the different ways by which children can now be exploited nowadays.

The effects in children can vary from person to person, and are also dependent upon the extent to which they were bullied. For instance, some children do not hold grudges as much, and are likely to forgive and forget much sooner than others, especially if they weren't bullied as much as others. Others however, might not be so willing. There are children who harbor within them the desire to gain revenge upon their bullies in some way or another. These people are focused upon getting to their bullies even years after school has ended. Some also suffer from clinical depression, which is a major problem amongst children who have been bullied extensively over the course of their school lives.

CHAPTER 4: WHO IS AT RISK?

Although, at first glance, it might seem as if bullies generally tend to select their victims at random, this is not the case actually. Revisions of historical cases of bullying as well as a basic understanding of the human mind provides in depth information about the mindsets of bullies, as well as the type of victims that they usually like to prey on. A bully would want to focus on those who pose little to no threat. Remember, on the inside, every bully is usually a coward, and when they do take a tumble, it is usually a hard fall. Therefore, these bullies are actually quite cautious when it comes to finding other children to bully.

Obviously, students who are more focused on their studies and aren't really outgoing and have weak physiques are at the greatest risk of being bullied. These students usually do not have a lot of friends; only around a couple or so.

As a result of that, they are not very forthcoming about their problems, and do not prefer sharing them with others either. More importantly, they also suffer from a lack of confidence, which makes them the perfect targets for bullies. A bully will usually know that this kid isn't going to make a lot of fuss when bullied, because their confidence levels are very low already. As a result of this, the bully is likely to prey on such kids since they prove to be the perfect targets; they are not going to tell anyone, and the bully can get whatever he or she wants from them.

Other children who are also at risk of being bullied include those children who are introverts or reserved. Those children who do not prefer to spend a lot of time in the company of others are likely to be subjected to bullying, both psychological and physiological over a longer period of time. Again, this is because of the fact that bullies find it much easier to prey on those who have a lower amount of confidence, which indicates that they are unable to stand up to their rights and can be intimidated quite easily. Ultimately, this works in the favor of the bully because such students aren't even willing to tell their own parents about what is happening to them.

Students who are proactive in sports and other activities that keep them fit are significantly less prone to being bullied, though a lot of such students eventually end up becoming bullies during their school, as well as professional careers. This is primarily because they begin to think of themselves as being superior to others, both in physicality as well as intellectually.

Similar to a bully, these people form very high opinions of themselves. The reason why other bullies stay off them hence becomes obvious: they are both similar to each other. A bully can make use of virtually anything in order to ridicule and downgrade another party. Ranging from calling names to stealing identifying information, bullies generally do not stop at anything until someone takes a stand against them. And because fear and lack of confidence grips most people, they are usually loath to taking a stand against bullies.

For parents, it is vitally important that they keep a close eye on the behavior of their child. Most of the time, parents overlook the most blatant signs that their child is being bullied, thinking that it is a 'part of growing up.' If your child is being bullied, it will not only affect his studies, but it will really cause a damaging impact on his whole life. From extracurricular activities to class performance, your child is going to see a dip in all of those. Again, it would be best if you start trying to raise the confidence of your kid from a very early age, as that helps significantly in making sure that they are able to stand up to bullies.

CHAPTER 5: BYSTANDERS

In virtually all incidents of bullying, a victim comes across bystanders. Bystanders are those people who are looking at what is happening to another student, but refuse to take notice or interfere to prevent it. Sadly, from childhood to adulthood, if a person is being wronged in public, there are always bystanders who refuse to take notice. Most of the time, it is because they are simply not interested in interfering in the matters of somebody else. That is, until the same thing happens to them. And, it usually does in the case of bullies.

If your child is being bullied in front of bystanders and nobody takes any notice, it is likely that he will become disillusioned with the people in his school. You might see a lack of friends, as he is likely to think that nobody is his actual 'friend.' That is one of the primary reasons for becoming isolated from a bigger group, causing problems in the long run.

The whole concept of being a bystander is wrong enough, yet it prevails throughout every age group of our life. If there are ten people watching one kid getting bullied, surely all ten of them could easily take down the bully in one go? Yet, they are all scared, quietly watching. This is the effect of fear that is instilled in them by the bully; they are so gripped by it that each of them, in their own minds, fears for their own safety. And that is the reason why nobody takes action.

However, if you happen to know of somebody who has seen bullying incidents and has refused to act to stop them from happening, it is unlikely that they'll be mentally at peace. Most people are often laden with guilt and remorse because of the fact that they could have done something to prevent the incident, yet refused to do so. As a result, they try to show an overly friendly attitude towards the victim, in an attempt to make them feel welcome and support them.

Yet, most of the time, it usually doesn't work out that way. The fact is that bystanders exist in all parts of life. From the time that we are kids to the time that we are adults in working professional jobs, there are always those who like to 'enjoy watching the show.' As a result, it is usually a wise idea to not look too deep in to it, since not everybody can be expected to come to your aid when the situation demands it.

CHAPTER 6: THOSE WHO BULLY

Those children who bully others have extremely distinctive characteristics as compared to normal children, and are often quite rebellious and dangerous in most respects. Usually, in 99 percent of the cases, those who resort to bullying usually come from very tough circumstances and often see home violence, as well as anger and continuous physiological torture. In an attempt to escape their lowly image at their homes, these children try to act all intimidating and angry at school. Led on by the backing off of other students, they eventually turn towards bullying in an attempt to vent their frustrations. Here are some of the most common characteristics of those who resort to bullying:

- Most of the children usually come from dysfunctional families. It is likely that they have been witness to first hand violence and aggression at their homes, and agree with it too. Most bullies usually hold a fairly positive image of the use of aggression in order to solve problems, and as a result do not really bother with other approaches.

- Children who are involved in bullying may find it a lot of fun to hit or push other children. Usually, these children are very adept at hitting those who are smaller than them, because a bully is seldom likely to take on students who are his size, in fear of losing. As a result, they prey on the fear of smaller children, and are very frequent with their hitting and use of pushing and intimidation.

- Bullies are usually physically much stronger than an average student. In most cases, bullies do not have a sculpted body, but instead have an oversized one so that they can use their 'hulking frame' in order to intimidate other students in to bending to their will. A lot of the people who are involved in bullying are overweight, and tend to consume a lot of food, most of which comes from the lunch boxes of other students.

- Perhaps the most obvious characteristic of bullies is the fact that very few students would actually regard themselves to be pleased in their company. And even those that do find themselves in the company of a bully are likely to be saying it because of fear of getting picked on later on. As a result, it is obvious that children of the same age do not hold a very high opinion of bullies, and rightly so. That is one of the prime reasons why most bullies do not have a good group of friends, and the ones that do befriend them are those who are in it for personal gain.

- Another obvious characteristic of bullies is the fact that they find it very troublesome to adhere to basic rules and guidelines. Since a bully considers himself to be 'superior' than most others, his mind leads him to believe that he is not liable to follow the rules and guidelines set for the average student. As a result, most bullies are unlikely to follow simple guidelines.

Usually, bullying comes as a result of what they have seen or been through. Most bullies are not exactly born as bullies from day one. Instead, their situation forces them to take a stand, and because they ultimately begin to enjoy forcing others to their will, they refuse to stop so quickly. Most of the children who are involved in bullying in early parts of their childhood and school life are often at a very high risk of suffering from failure in school, and are likely to dropout of school altogether. Ultimately, the chances of these people committing criminal acts in the later years of their lives are also very high.

For most parents, it is important to keep a check on their child to ensure that he or she is not involved in bullying other students. Most of the time, professional counseling can prove to be a very important factor in helping students get rid of their bullying habits, and also allows them to become a lot more peaceful and focused, hence also helping their studies in the long run. However, since most parents usually choose to ignore such obvious traits of their child, it often becomes troublesome and tends to grow, causing problems in the latter years of a child's life.

CHAPTER 7: SUICIDE OR BULLYCIDE

Will a person actually commit suicide after being bullied? Is there any extent to the amount of bullying that a person can bear? The answer to both of these questions, is sadly, yes. The term bullycide was first coined in 2001 by Tim Field and Neil Marr, in a book they wrote regarding bullying. In it, they describe bullycide as the committing of suicide after being bullied via physical abuse or on social media, which ultimately leads the victims to become disillusioned with life, and finally end it.

Now, some will argue that bullycide should also be attributable to the bully, who should be regarded as the killer in this regard. After all, if it wasn't for the continuous harassment and torture that the bully inflicted on these children, they would still be amongst us, right? Unfortunately, several states do not even have basic laws against bullying. Only recently, the United States passed bills that actually set up prosecution laws against bullies and how to deal with them. The term became more famous in 2010, when numerous children in the United States committed suicide after being bullied to various extents.

One of the terms that has become hugely popular in the past few years is cyberbullying. Cyberbullying is basically the bullying of somebody over the internet, primarily using social media. Since the rise of Facebook and other social websites have become hugely common, most people find it to be an extremely easy task to leak out information. In the case of Amanda Todd, as was mentioned earlier in the book, her bully made a false profile and then added all of her friends, and distributed compromising pictures of her on the internet.

Constant bullying can really alter the effect one's life, and in some cases, victims may eventually end up committing suicide unless they are given proper means of handling the situation. Being able to deal with cyberbullying is not really difficult, though parents need to make sure that they are able to find out whether their child is going through such a problem or not.

Over the past few years, suicide has become a major problem in relation to bullying. It was one of the primary reasons why bills were passed in the United States in order to prevent bullying from spreading any further, and legal action is now threatened against those bullies who can be caught in time. Unfortunately, such bullies are seldom caught; out of fear of getting beat up, children do not speak up against them.

However, a simple look at the statistics is enough to show that bullycide rates are rising; more and more children are resorting to end their lives rather than report or fight against the constant harassment. Schools are also failing to provide protection to such students, as most of the bullying is done outside of the school premises, where the bullies find it much easier to pick on others. Most of the victims of bullying suffer in silence, going through mental torture and pondering over the importance of their life, until they may consider suicide to be a final resort.

There are however, ways by which you can find out whether your child is contemplating suicide or not. Here are a few characteristics to look out for:

1. The first major sign is the fact that a child is likely to become preoccupied with death. If you find that your child is bringing death in to conversation quite often, it is likely a result of the fact that he or she is contemplating it. Most children who are occupied with death will generally begin to express their desire in terms of writing or drawing, sending out a clear message. If your child isn't very trusting towards you, then you

need to keep an eye out for such signs.

2. The most obvious way by which children express their desire to commit suicide is by making suicidal statements. If you hear your child make suicidal statements all the time, it is likely because suicide has been a factor on his mind quite often. Most parents often tend to ignore such statements because they consider their children to be quite volatile on an emotional level. However, such signs should never be ignored, and instead, parents

should try and talk to the child to get them help.

3. Another major sign that your child is contemplating suicide is when he or she begins to give away their belongings. As a result of the constant bullying, most children who make up their minds to commit suicide generally first start by giving away their belongings to others before finally killing themselves. It is the responsibility of parents to make sure that they keep a track on their children and see whether they have begun giving

away stuff that was previously important to them.

4. Most children who have made up their minds to commit suicide are known to have quite hostile behaviors towards friends and family. At first, they become completely withdrawn from both their social circles as well as family gathering. They are not interested in meeting with others, nor are they interested in making new friends. If another person does take the initiative to meet up or befriend them, these people are likely to

respond with hostility. As a result of the constant mental stress that they suffer, most of the children are observed to develop quite angry moods. They become silent most of the time, and rather than involve themselves in other matters, choose to remain on the sides.

There are numerous other signs that parents can take note of. For instance, running away from home is one of the most obvious signs that your child is contemplating suicide, especially if the environment at home is perfectly normal. Secondly, if your child suddenly begins to neglect personal appearance, it is possible he or she has lost the will to live, and is looking to commit suicide. For parents, such warning signs should serve as major indicators in order to take the right step immediately. Rather than let your child suffer, it is a wise idea to take the right steps to get help.

There are suicide hotlines, as well as psychiatric clinics in which your child can receive therapy. More importantly, finding out about their bullying incidents and putting a stop to them can also serve as a major way of preventing your child from committing suicide.

CHAPTER 8: PREVENTION

Prevention against bullying and bullycide are both very important nowadays. Ever since the numerous laws that were set in place regarding bullying in the United States, a number of organizations have sprouted up in order to provide awareness to parents, as well as build up the confidence of children to fight against the constant bullying.

Several websites have also been created, which are focused on providing anonymous reports against bullies, as well as what children can do to prevent themselves from getting bullied. Only recently, a cyberbully was stopped from harassing a girl in Florida when the authorities traced down his social media page, and then arrested him at his house, shutting down his efforts and his page in the progress.

Ever since the high profile suicides in 2010, the government has become quite proactive in dealing with bullies. Numerous schools have sponsored organizations that are created by and run by students. However, a member of the committee is a teacher as well, which means that action can be taken against bullies. Students usually meet up within the school premises, holding meetings regarding different bullies in their schools.

These forums provide people with a chance to take a stand against bullying. Since most students are generally loath to speaking up against bullying, these forums provide them with a platform to take a step against bullying in the long run. It allows them to actually have a say, and have their voice heard. More importantly, giving students an open platform to discuss their opinions is a very important and healthy part of a school lifestyle nowadays, as it allows them to take steps in order to rectify the situation.

There are dedicated groups on top social media websites, such as Facebook and Reddit, that allow people to carry out discussions regarding bullying in their schools, as well as the preventive measures that can be taken in order to combat it.

CHAPTER 9:
CYBERBULLYING

Ever since the rise of the social media, bullying has taken a whole new step forward. Previously, bullying was generally carried out in isolated corridors or empty classrooms. In a handful of cases, the bully would go towards public embarrassment. Now, thanks to cyber and social media, bullying has taken a whole new level. People are now bullied and threatened over the internet. Again, we point to the case of Amanda Todd, who was a prime victim of cyberbullying.

The person who bullied her had somehow gotten ahold of some compromising pictures of her, and had threatened to distribute them to the public.

Amanda changed schools several times throughout her young life, but every time, the bully would find her Facebook profile, and then make friends with her new classmates. At the end of the day, the bully would anonymously send out those compromising pictures and videos to her new friends, eventually causing a rift. After suffering through immense pain and psychological torture, Amanda Todd decided to commit suicide.

As horrific as this is, it is a

prime example of how bad cyberbullying can prove to be. In some cases, cyberbullying is much worse than actual, physical bullying. This is because even though physical bullying can be traced to the person, most of the time the cyberbully is an anonymous person who is spreading false or compromising information regarding the victim. This means that the victim generally has no idea about who is spreading all of this compromising information against him or her.

As a result, tracing them down and getting them apprehended becomes an uphill task. There is no doubt that cyberbullying can take a major toll upon students. However, numerous websites are also present on the internet that provide healthy advice against how to deal with cyberbullies. Social media websites have also created an option to 'report' incidents that might be affecting the integrity of a person, making it much easier for people to send out a complaint against their cyberbully.

Previously, cyberbullying was obviously not as widely popular as it is now. At present, cyberbullying has reached a whole new level due to the rise in the sales of smart phones. Virtually every other student is connected online via their smart phones, and the transfer of information takes place at a rapid rate. As a result, even a small 'status' by an anonymous person can prove to cause widespread damage to the reputation of another person in the long run. Hence, it is easy to say that cyberbullying has become a terrible feature of society, one that needs to be dealt with in the highest order to make sure that people do not resort to it in the long run.

CHAPTER 10: SOCIAL MEDIA AND CRIMINALS

There's no denying that social media can be a good thing. It helps us to keep in touch with our friends, share opinions, and even publicize our work. Many people have found new job opportunities, long-lost relatives and even the love of their lives via the power of social media.

Yet this relatively new phenomenon has also led to an unprecedented rise in internet-related crime and it would seem that the world of social media has in fact opened up a world of opportunity for criminals looking for victims. We have all heard the reports of internet related fraud and of course, bullying via social media and these issues are worrying enough, but statistics also show a dangerous trend for stalkers, sex abusers, and even serial killers using social media as a way to locate potential targets.

With social media use on the rise and more and more people, particularly the younger generation, signing up to different sites every day, it is vital that we become aware of these crimes - and what we can do to protect ourselves.

An estimated 81 percent of internet crime is currently related to a social media site. That's a scary statistic. It's also believed that around one million people become victims of some form of cyber crime every day. Although a large percentage of this is made up of crimes such as identity theft, fraud and internet scams, when it comes to the social media side of things, the crimes become even more serious. Up to 33 percent of internet related sex crimes were in some way instigated through the use of a social networking site and indeed, sex crimes are the most common of social media related crimes, all too often involving minors. Police believe that as many as half of recently convicted sex offenders have used social media to track down or get close to their intended victims.

Social media can also influence physical crime, as potential burglars use information posted by victims to determine when they are going to be away from home. An estimated 50 percent of potential burglars use social media in this way, so what seems like an innocent comment to friends about an upcoming holiday can have sinister repercussions. Even violent crimes can be instigated on social media, and cyberbullying can escalate into something far more physical.

In Florida a young female victim of cyberbullying sustained serious injuries after the cyberbullies tracked her down and subjected her to a beating. They were later arrested for assault and the victim was compensated for her injuries, but of course for victims of such crime, no amount of compensation can ever truly be enough.

In 2008, a young girl was shot by another girl after being hounded and threatened by her via social media. What seems to be at first a 'faceless' crime can clearly escalate into something far more violent.

So how can you keep yourself and your children safe on social media? With such shocking statistics it would be easy to assume that the best option would be to not engage with social media at all, but for many people in today's internet age this is neither practical nor desirable. Instead, taking sensible precautions when using social media can drastically reduce your chances of being a target for criminals prowling social media sites. Firstly, whatever social networking sites you belong to, familiarize yourself with their privacy and security settings to ensure that the personal settings on your profile are offering you maximum security on your site, so that as much of your information as possible is limited only to those you want to see it. Perhaps most importantly, be very selective with the information you post, regardless of your privacy settings. It is advisable not to include your address, date of birth, phone number, and any photos that clearly show your house, place of work, or favorite haunts.

For teenage girls in

particular, don't post provocative photos or accept 'friends' whose identity you are not completely sure of. Don't let your online friends know your every movement.

Although social media has given rise to related crime, it has however also proved useful in the tackling of that crime. Many law enforcement agencies are now active on social media sites, which can also provide another avenue for those anonymously wanting to report a crime. Undercover officers have used social media sites to lure and catch pedophiles and sex offenders, and other criminals have, somewhat ironically perhaps, been tracked down through their own social networking profiles.

CHAPTER 11: PEER PRESSURE

For a lot of students, peer pressure plays a major role. The common definition of peer pressure is primarily the influence caused by another peer, or a group that causes another student to change their behavior, their values and their outlook on life. For instance, whereas a student might have reported the bullying incident that they have been a victim of previously, a peer might change their decision making process by calling them a 'telltale.' Since they do not want to be referred to as a telltale, they are unlikely to file a complaint.

No matter how you look at it, the sad fact is that a lot of students succumb to peer pressure. Everybody wants to be remain at the top, but very few of the students are actually able to break from the mold and think outside of the box, without having to worry about peer pressure all the time. Unfortunately, peer pressure is a very major part of our daily lives, and we give it value over rational thinking.

In a school environment, peer pressure can play a major role. Students do not report major crimes just because they are under pressure from their peers not to. Bystanders who are witness to severe acts of bullying also refuse to report such incidents due to peer pressure. Nobody likes to be considered a social outcast, which is what they would be called if they complain about the bully. As a result, many students tend to just stay quiet, silently observing the events that take place around them without actually filing a complaint against them.

It is the responsibility of parents to make sure that they instill in their child the belief and confidence that is required to deal with peer pressure and not succumb to it. If a child is confident enough, he will not bother with peer pressure, and will instead take decisions that he values on his own. However, for a child lacking in confidence, he is likely to succumb to peer pressure quite early, and just 'go along with the flow' throughout the rest of his life and career.

CHAPTER 12: HOW TO GET HELP

For children and for parents of children who are bullied, getting help is not really a difficult problem anymore. A simple search on the internet reveals numerous websites that are focused on providing assistance to victims of bullying, both physiological and psychological. If your child has been bullied extensively and requires psychological assistance, one of the best options available is to take him or her to the local psychologist. Most psychologists are very well trained in dealing with traumatizing situations and can provide rational explanations and help with decision making that will help put your child's mind at ease.

More importantly, there are also a handful of different websites that provide information to parents regarding the steps that they need to take in order to recuperate the mental health of their child. For instance, one of the easiest things that parents can do is to sit around and talk with their child. Rather than ignoring daily matters, a wise idea is to hold a discussion on a daily basis about how school life is going, and how the child is coping. This allows the child to get a lot off his mind in just one go, allowing him to feel free on the inside.

Depending upon the state that you are currently living in, there are different ways to get help. For instance, in Florida, there is an official website against bullying which aims to take strong steps against bullying. There are numerous ways by which a report can be filed on the website, allowing you to highlight the bully and bring him to justice.

Most students who have been victims to bullying for long periods of time generally require a psychologist in order to get psychotherapy sessions, which are aimed at strengthening their hearts and their muscles. Needless to say, getting help against bullying has become a much easier prospect than it was a decade ago. Whereas people had to quietly approach their parents or their teachers to file a complaint against bullying, all they have to do now is to just log on to the internet and highlight the matter at the official forums of their school. Most forums have dedicated discussion threads against bullying, hence allowing students to express their problems, either by being named or by remaining anonymous.

Apart from this, numerous non governmental organizations (NGOs) have also taken up the mantle to reduce bullying. A number of NGOs have been created that focus on bullying exclusively and provide relief efforts such as psychotherapy sessions as well as complaint centers and parents alike to fie their complaints against bullying.

More importantly, these organizations also provide a very positive response to bullying by actually talking it out with the bully, understanding their problems and providing them with proper treatment, hence ensuring a healthy outlook in the long run.

CHAPTER 13: ANTI BULLYING LAWS

The United States is home to a lot of bullies. There are comprehensive anti-bullying laws that have been passed throughout the United States, and forty-nine states have actually passed anti-bullying legislation. The first state to pass anti-bullying legislation was Georgia, back in 1999. The only state that does not have any anti-bullying laws is Montana.

The government has also created a watchdog organization

in order to get reports and headlines regarding bullying, and the "Bully Police USA" provides dedicated information to the government regarding all new cases of bullying to the government. Then, government officials take notice of the bullying incidents that take place, and decide whether legal action should be pursued on them or not.

Obviously, controversy is rife as a result of the laws that were passed. Whereas previously people were only bullied due to their physical and mental weaknesses, children have resorted to different kinds of bullying in schools, such as bullying due to their religious beliefs, bullying the LGBT community, bullying due to race and ethnicity, and there are also laws that make bullying against teachers an official crime.

Several laws have also been put in place regarding cyberbullying, which is a rapidly increasing problem nowadays. As more and more children are subjected to psychological abuse over the internet, the government has decided to take notice and make it an official crime.

The spreading of hurtful or demeaning material regarding another student has also been prohibited completely, and students have been asked to report such cases to the local authorities immediately.

As mentioned, anti-bullying laws have been passed in 49 of the

50 states within the United States, which means that bullying is regarded as a serious problem by the government and rightly so. These laws were generally brought about in the past couple of years only. After the high profile deaths of numerous teenagers within the United States in 2010, which managed to cause an uproar in the industry, there was bound to be a strong reaction by the government. The death of Amanda Todd in 2012 also led to an acceleration of the whole process, as bullying was actively recognized and regarded as a crime.

Throughout the U.S., the definitions of cyberbullying and bullying have been laid out in explicit detail. Thanks to the support societies that have been created by the government, filing a complaint is just as easy as filling out a form, making it easier for parents and children to get help when they need it the most.

Moreover, NGOs actively tour the country and hold seminars in different schools and vicinities in order to provide awareness to the students regarding the dangers of not speaking out against bullying of any kind, and also urge students to speak out in detail regarding who they were bullied by as well as how. Perhaps the most important factor in this regard is the fact that local authorities are now involved in combating all kinds of cyberbullying. If you have been bullied in person and choose to file a complaint, the police have probable cause to arrest a bully and ask him to confess. If not, a full-fledged investigation goes underway in order to determine the rights and wrongs.

These minor changes prove to be very helpful in the long run as they are aimed at bringing out confidence in the students to combat the situations. For a lot of students who are bullied because of their ethnicity, race, or sexual orientation, the government provides active protection by even issuing out restraint orders against certain individuals if constant complaints are being filed.

Cyberbullying is also dealt with in the same effective manner as a result of the new laws, which provide maximum relief to students who are constantly victimized. For any student who is being bullied by another, it is a very important step in their life to actually file a complaint against it. Not filing a complaint means that you are not only destroying your own life by forcing yourself to suffer through the constant torture and mental agony, but you are also taking no steps to provide a positive change in the bully as well.

CHAPTER 14: SCHOOL AND CAMPUS RESPONSBILITIES

It is the responsibility of the school to make sure that the school actively tracks students who are involved in the cases of bullying. Teachers and staff need to keep an eye out during the recess or during class time in order to discover bullying incidents. The school also needs to identify bullies and take appropriate steps in order to reprimand them.

More importantly, it also falls

within the responsibilities of the school to make sure that they provide a platform for bullied children to speak up against the act.

If a school allows for collective retaliation against an activity, very few bullies will actually exist. Most of the schools have created forums on their official websites that allow students to highlight acts of bullying as well as those who were involved, allowing the school authorities to investigate further. Moreover, it is also the responsibility of the school to set up therapy sessions for students who are bullied on their premises. Unless students are actually encouraged to speak up against bullying and share their experiences, most of them would stay silent on such matters and take no steps to rectify the situation, which means they are constantly suffering from mental torture.

CHAPTER 15: STATISTICS

The stats against bullying do not paint a very pretty picture, as it just shows the rise of bullying, as well as the influence that it holds in students at present. Here are some interesting stats related to bullying:

- According to the National Education Association, it is estimated that around 160,000 children generally avoid going to school because they are unable to deal with their bullies.

- In American schools, the approximate number of bullies is around 2.1 million. According to the National School Safety Center, around 2.7 million students are victims of bullying.

- One in every 7 students in Grade 12 can be regarded as either a bully, or has suffered from bullying.

- Bystanders are also quite common, as stats show that around 56 percent of students have been first hand witnesses to some form of bullying.

- Each month, around 262,000 students are attacked physically in secondary schools.

- An estimated 15 percent of all types of absenteeism is based directly due to fears of being bullied.

- Shockingly, 90 percent of the students who were surveyed from the fourth through eighth grade reported that they have suffered from some type of bullying in their life.

- According to The Boston Globe, since March 2002, around 15 students between the ages of 11 to 14 have committed suicide in Massachusetts as a result of bullying.

- Over the past three decades, the suicide rates have increased by more than 50 percent amongst young teenagers, primarily due to a result of increased bullying.

- In 2005, the total number of children who decided to commit suicide after being bullied amounted to 270. These were children primarily between the ages of 11 to 14 years of age.

It is easy to see the impact that bullying can have on a young child, and how it can cause such widespread damage to their whole lives. It is our social responsibility to make sure that we root it out and make sure it stops hurting the growth of young children throughout the globe.

CHAPTER 16: TRUE STORIES OF BULLYCIDE

One child to die because of bullying, abuse, harassment or for any other tormenting anguish is too many.

Kenneth Weishuhn

In 2012, Kenneth Weishuhn, a gay high school freshman from Paullina, Iowa, took his own life after being bullied by classmates at school, online, and with death threats by phone.

The bullying began with an anti-gay Facebook group, created by Kenneth's classmates. His mother, Jeannie Chambers, said she knew her son was being harassed, and said that her son told her, "Mom, you don't know how it feels to be hated."

According to his sister Kayla, the abuse that started after he "came out" was from people he had trusted: "People that were originally his friends, they kind of turned on him. A lot of people, they either joined in or were too scared to say anything."

Amanda Todd

When she was in the 7th grade, Amanda Todd met a man in an online chat room who talked her into flashing him her breasts. A year later, the man contacted her on Facebook and asked her to 'put on a show' for him. He threatened to release a picture of her to everyone she knew if she did not comply with his wishes.

He knew her address, her name, where she went to school, and who her friends and family members were. Amanda's pictures were released and went viral. Other kids at her school saw the pictures and started to bully and tease her. She became severely depressed, developed anxiety and began to use drugs and alcohol. A year later, after she changed schools and found a new group of friends, the man came back and created a Facebook page, using her topless photo as his profile picture.

Her new friends started ignoring her, talking about her, and bullying her. She later revealed her feelings in a video she recorded and posted on YouTube, describing how she cried every night and lost all her friends. Around this time, Amanda began cutting herself.

Again, Amanda changed schools, where a boy flirted with her. As a result, girls from the first school came to her new school and beat her up, while people watched and filmed it. She later revealed, "I was left all alone and left on the ground." After the beating, she managed to find her way to the road, where she lied down in a ditch. Her father found her there.

When Amanda returned home, she tried to commit suicide by drinking bleach. Once again, she moved to a new city, but the bullying continued. Therapy, combined with anti-depressants, did little to help her depression and anxiety, and she continued to cut herself and attempted suicide again. Then in September 2012 Amanda wrote her story on flashcards and recorded her video that she later posted on YouTube.

Amanda's body was found at

her home in British Columbia, Canada on October 10, 2012.

Hannah Smith

Hannah Smith, a 14-year-old girl from Lutterworth, Leicestershire, England, hanged herself in her bedroom on August 3, 2013. Her body was discovered by her older sister.

In the weeks leading up to her death, Hannah had been subjected to cruel taunts and insults about her weight and a family death on Ask.fm, a question-and-answer social networking site that allows anonymous participation. Bullies on Ask.fm urged her to drink bleach and cut herself. According to Hannah's father, she went to Ask.fm to look for advice on the skin condition eczema.

After her death, Hannah's father found a note that read: "As I sit here day by day I wonder if it's going to get better. I want to die, I want to be free. I can't live like this any more. I'm not happy."

Following the suicide, Hannah's older sister, Jo, described how, just days after discovering her younger sister's body, she started receiving abusive messages on Facebook mocking her loss and blaming her grieving father's parenting skills for the tragic death.

Rachael Neblett

Rachael Neblett, a seventeen-year-old high school student from Kentucky began receiving threatening emails through her MySpace account in the summer of 2006. The anonymous emails were of a stalking terroristic nature.

Rachael's parents brought the emails to the attention of the principal of her high school. As the emails included details of her movements during class and after school, it was obvious that the bully was another student at the school.

In October Rachael received an email stating, "I am not going to put you in the hospital, I am going to put you in the morgue." After receiving that email, Rachael did not want to go to school or go out with her friends. On October 9, shortly after receiving the threatening email, Rachael took her own life.

Peyton, Rachael's older sister wrote: *"My little sister committed suicide October 9, 2006. Her name is Rachael Neblett. I am here to tell you a little about her. She was 17 when she died, and the most amazing girl you would ever meet. She was an out-going, loving, and caring person. You would never dream that she would do that to herself...She was not just my sister, she was my best friend...All I have now is a big, black hole where my heart was. Because my little sister is gone, I*

won't be able to see her anymore--
no more trips to the mall, no more
smiles, hugs, late movie nights,
nothing. It's gone."

Jessica Logan

Jessica Logan was a petite, blond-haired, blue-eyed Ohio high school senior who committed suicide after sexting a nude photo of herself to her boyfriend. When they broke up, he sent the photo to everyone else at her school. Jessie was cruelly harassed for months by the other girls at her school, who called her a slut and a whore. When Jessie's grades dropped, she started skipping school and when she did go to school, she would hide in the bathroom to avoid being teased.

Jessie decided to tell her story on a Cincinnati television station. Her purpose was simple: "I just want to make sure no one else will have to go through this again." The interview was in May 2008. Two months later, on July 3, 2008, Jessie attended the funeral of a boy who had committed suicide, then came home and killed herself.

Her mother found her hanging in the closet with Jessie's cell phone on the floor nearby.

True stories of cyberbullying

http://www.noplace4hate.org/real-stories-about-bullying/

"My thoughts and prayers are with Kenneth, Amanda, Hannah, Jessica, Rachael and their families. These a just a few of many that were bullied and ridiculed, and who found it too difficult to deal with being harassed and bullied. May God Bless you all."

RJ

About the Author

RJ **Parker**, Ph.D., is an award-winning and bestselling true crime author and owner of RJ Parker Publishing, Inc. He has written over 30 true crime books which are available in eBook, paperback and audiobook editions and have sold in over 100 countries. He holds certifications in Serial Crime, Criminal Profiling and a Ph.D. in Criminology.

To date, RJ has donated over 3,000 autographed books to allied troops serving overseas and to our wounded warriors recovering in Naval and Army hospitals all over the world. He also donates to Victims of Violent Crimes Canada.

Contact Information

Author's Email:

AuthorRJParker@gmail.com

Publisher's Email:

Agent@RJParkerPublishing.com

Website:

http://RJPARKERPUBLISHING.com/

Twitter:

http://www.Twitter.com/realRJParker

Facebook:

https://www.Facebook.com/AuthorRJParker

Instagram:

https://Instagram.com/RJParkerPub

Bookbub:

https://www.bookbub.com/authors/rj-parker

Amazon Author's Page:

rjpp.ca/RJ-PARKER-BOOKS

www.ingramcontent.com/pod-product-compliance
Lightning Source LLC
Chambersburg PA
CBHW050533280326
41933CB00011B/1571